Sarah Shedd, A. P. Howe

**Poems of Sarah Shedd**

Founder of the Shedd Free Library, Washington, N.H.

Sarah Shedd, A. P. Howe

**Poems of Sarah Shedd**
*Founder of the Shedd Free Library, Washington, N.H.*

ISBN/EAN: 9783337285586

Printed in Europe, USA, Canada, Australia, Japan

Cover: Foto ©Lupo / pixelio.de

More available books at **www.hansebooks.com**

# POEMS
OF
# Sarah Shedd,
## FOUNDER
of the
## Shedd Free Library,
WASHINGTON, N. H.

Arranged and Compiled by A. P. HOWE.

WASHINGTON, N. H.
PRINTED BY F. H. HOWE.
*1883.*

## INTRODUCTION.

This little volume is presented to the public with the utmost confidence that it will meet with universal favor, not only from the personal friends and intimate acquaintances of Miss Shedd, but from the general public, and especially from all who have been, are, or ever will be the patrons of the Free Public Library which she has, with such liberality of heart, and magnanimity of soul, bequeathed to her native town.

Miss Shedd's poems need no interpretation. They are simple truths, told in a simple, yet eloquent manner. They come from the heart, and go straight to the heart of every one who has any affinity with the nobility of thouhgt, and the high tone of moral rectitude, that pervades every line of her writings, and invests them with a dignity and sacredness of purpose, that commands not only the respect, but the esteem of all who come within the radius of her influence. Not only lofty, but they possess the freshness of the morning breeze when it steals into our chamber and wakes us by its gentle breath to new life and vigor.

Her writings require no gilded paper to make them attractive, for they shine with a brilliancy all their own: not such as dazzles with a glaring light, but like the pure scintillations of a star of the first magnitude, sparkling and pure, brilliant yet modest, reflecting as from a polished mirror the intrinsic excellence of her mind and character.

Deeming it might be of interest to the general reader, and especially to those who never had the pleasure of a personal acquaintance with Miss Shedd, we append a few lines eulogistic of her life and character, suggested by such communications as we have been able to obtain from those who knew her best. We reproduce the following letter received by the compiler, which will be found to be eminently suggestive, having omitted such passages as possess nothing of interest to the public.

Hillsboro' Upper Village, N. H. May 24th, 1882.
Mr. A. P. Howe,

Dear Sir. The only memento of Miss Shedd in my possession is a small painting upon an album leaf accompanied by these lines:—

A rose, dear Almira, love is the token;
May'st thou keep its petals unbroken;
Ray after ray of its beauty will depart;
A lesson humbly learn and cultivate the heart.

\* \* \* \* \* \* \* \*

"Many of her writings are doubtless lost, for the reason, she herself set small value upon them, they fell so short of her high ideals.

"Contrary to the impressions of many she never made either writing or teaching, a profession. I trust the cittizens of her native town may appreciate this gifted, heroic, and self-sacrificing woman none the less, if they know that the legacy she left them was earned by hard and constant toil, for many years in the mills of Lowell, Biddiford, and Salem. Her employment was 'dressing' which used to be done in the upper stories of the mills, and besides being the most laborious work done by female operatives, it necessitated the climbing of many flights of stairs. She told me that in the last days of her factory life, she was often obliged to help herself in ascending them with her hands, and to stop many times to rest. Few of her most intimate friends knew the painful and trying circumstances which condemned her to this obscure and laborious life, when she was so fitted by nature to have distinguished herself in any literary or artistic profession to which her taste or ambition urged her.

\* \* \* \* \* \* \* \*

"In 1861 she mentioned to me her plan of founding a Public Library. All her life she had toiled and thought of others, had lived for an object, that object had been to do good; 'How,' she said, 'can this money be put to the best use?'

"I think she thought solely of that, and never of any fame or honor it would bring to herself,

"She was an ardent lover of good books and the few she bought were an index of her mind and taste; and a library such as she contemplated, and would have selected, would, indeed, be an inestimable boon to any community.

"She had a mind of great strength and versatility, and, notwithstanding her laborious life, she had found time to store it well with knowledge. She loved music and poetry, but took the greatest delight in ethical and philosophical studies. From specimens of her painting I have seen, I believe she might have become an artist of no mean rank.

"She had a kindly and affectionate disposition, a high sense of honor, and sterling common sense.

"Her personal appearance was no more ordinary than her mind. Her portrait gives one a good idea of her face, except that her hair was very dark. She had neither regular features or a fine complexion, but her face was very winning. She was above the medium highth and always and everywhere had an inborn dignity, grace, and self-possession that might have become any Duchess.

"She was a good conversationalist, and when she spoke every one listened. It is needless to say such a person would be at home with all intelligent and well bred persons; and by them she was everywhere welcomed. All snobbery and pretence seemed to retire before this really noble woman. * * * * * * * * * *

"Very respectfully,

Charlotte J. Curtis."

She was eminently social in her disposition and nature; highly appreciative in her estimate of those with whom she came in contact; discriminating in her selection of associates and intimate acquaintances, yet a friend to all; keenly sympathizing with the laboring class, of which she was a representative and a noble example; liberal, almost to a fault, toward the weak and erring, yet never compromising with wrong: always looking into the little end of the telescope at her own faults, while the misdemeanors of others were seen at a distance and appeared small in comparison. She loved her Mother with a constancy and devotion that called forth the admiration of all, seeming to realize that to her she owed every thing worth possessing in life. Home to her was a sacred place and possessed a charm above every other earthly place. Her poems abound with touching and affectionate allusions to the place of her nativity, and, when far away from home, her thoughts would often turn to the scenes of her youth, and she seemed to—

> "Tread again its hills,
> And track its mossy rills
> With foot-steps light."*

She was a close student of Nature, and reveled in the luxuriant beauty of field and forest, medow and upland, lofty hill and fertile valley. She loved to commune with Nature, and would often sit under the over-hanging branches of a stately tree and listen to the hum of the bee, and the sweet song of bird, while she communed with her own thoughts, or penned the expresssive and beautiful lines a few of which have been preserved to deck these pages. And yet she was no idle dreamer, giving unrestrained flight to the wings of an untutored fancy, soar-

*See Page 38.

ing into the ethereal regions with a cometary flight far above the ken of mortal man, or launching upon an unknown sea, without chart or rudder or compass, to be torn, tossed, and discomfited by Passion's fearful tempest, or hopelessly engulphed in the maelstrom of Despair; but she was an earnest, unremitting worker; she dealt with the realities of life; with her, duty had not become an obsolete term; but with a scrupulous regard for its performance, she was ever on the alert to embrace every opportunity to assist those struggling with life's stern realities; sympathizing with the bereaved, whispering hope to the disconsolate, and lifting the load from the heart overburdened with grief.

But it is not alone for her blameless life, spotless character, and sympathetic nature, that we admire her and venerate her memory: it is not alone that she walked in the highway cast up for emancipated humanity, instead of groveling in the byways of sin: it is not alone that she sang of "lofty thought," "heroic deeds," or "life's stern duties nobly met," that her name will be handed down from father to son and become a familiar household word in homes made glad by the crowning act of her life.—

In the quiet village of Washington,

New Hampshire, a village of which its citizens may well be proud, stands a noble edifice, THE SHEDD FREE LIBRARY BUILDING, the gift of one of Washington's honored sons, made necessary by the munificent bequest of this noble, heroic, and truly gifted woman.

> Within these walls her angel form
> Shall float on golden wings,
> And feed the hungry soul on food
> That sweet contentment brings.
>
> O! breathe her name in accents soft,
> With reverence be it said;
> We venerate that goodly name,
> The sainted SARAH SHEDD.

Washington, N. H., April 20th, 1883.

## CONTENTS.

| | Page. |
|---|---|
| Old Draper Hill | 3 |
| The Old Box Pews | 6 |
| An Indian Maiden's Lament | 27 |
| Our Boston Joe | 28 |
| Thy Presence | 32 |
| To J. W. S. | 33 |
| I have woven a wreath | 34 |
| I miss thee my Mother | 35 |
| Impromptu | 37 |
| Stray Thoughts | 38 |
| I Wish I were Again a Child | 40 |
| To Ellen Cockrain | 42 |
| An Invitation &c. | 43 |
| Soliloquy of the Half-moon | 45 |
| The Yankee | 47 |
| Autumn Leaves | 50 |
| Gone— Mary A. | 51 |
| To M. G. on her Wedding Day | 53 |
| To Jennie | 53 |
| Picture No. 2 | 57 |
| Morning | 58 |
| My School Days | 59 |
| Crossing the Rappahannock | 61 |
| My old Cottage Home | 70 |
| A Poem | 72 |
| The Days when we went a Fishing | 74 |
| The Evergreen Tree | 76 |
| Obituary | 78 |
| Valentines | 80 to 88 |
| The Beautiful | 89 |

# Old Draper Hill.

Old Draper Hill! Old Draper Hill,
Peace throbbing heart, be still, be still.
What floods of memory through me thrill
At thy blest name, Old Draper Hill!

In life's young hours when called to rise,
For day sped up the eastern skies,
I turned me to thy forehead fair,
For morning broke in glory there.

How often since, I've climbed thy height
With friend so gay, of heart so light,
To drink the fragrant morning air,
Grandeur with beauty blending there.

Where e'er I turn with graphic eye,
Some hidden memory seems to lie,
The faces fade, the forms are still,
Thou art the same Old Draper Hill.

A grand old dome there Lovell lies
Piercing with rocky crest the skies;
While sleeping here a Mountain Lake
With every breeze will start and wake.

From out its breast a silver rill
Runs rippling round the dear old hill,
Whose strength and beauty handicraft
Compels to turn a ponderous shaft;

Where milk white cottages appear
And flowers their tender petals rear.
While from its bounds the rill is seen,
Winding along green banks between.

But raise there, eyes, Lo! mountains rise,
Whose lofty summits sweep the skies;
And grander still, see forests nod,
'Tis Nature's march with feet unshod.

A village here lies at my feet.
My native village, O! how sweet!
Here my young heart was taught to pray
And my young lips what words to say.

I've trod by sea, by mount, and been
Familiar in the haunts of men,
But dearest find the place and joys
Where childhood garnered up its toys.

The school house dear and village spire
Remind me of a youthful choir,
Whose voices as they trod thy hill
Could e'en the rocks with music thrill.

And where are they, that youthful band?
Some linger here—— to distant land
And clime remote, have others sped,
And some are with the blessed dead.

I see, I see tablet and shaft—
As onward still my eye I cast—
Can not I read their names from here?
What meaneth it, this falling tear.

O Weston: child and soul of song,
Thy brother too has joined the throng,
Heard are your harps still round this spot;
In death ye were divided not.

Sister and Mother, tender wife,
Were ye not types of the heavenly life?
While I repeat the name of Laws,
How your loved form my spirit awes.

And Millen, mimic of the grove,
Whose voice with bird and bee would rove;
M'Questen, Wilson, tell not ye
How the soul loveth when life's shadows flee!

But mine eye lingers, loth to part
From loved forms I've pressed heart to heart;
But I turn ever on, on to the right
Where the road, hills between, wanes out of sight.

Old Draper Hill! Old Draper Hill,
Peace throbbing heart, be still, be still.
What floods of memory through me thrill
At thy blest name, Old Draper Hill!

# ALL ABOUT THE DAYS OF THE OLD BOX PEWS.

### A POEM.

Read at the Fair of the Ladies' Sewing Circle connected with the Universalist Society in Washington, N. H., Nov. 8th, 1859.

Good ladies, and ye gentlemen,
   Give ear while I repeat
Some legends of our native town,
   The occasion seemeth meet—
How our grandfathers used to live:
   I hope it will be news,
And all about the days of yore,
   And of the old—Box Pews.

From Harvard yonder some there came,
   And some from Amherst plains,
From Westford and from old Braintree,
   Newton and Malbury lanes;
From other towns they also came,
   A number very great,
But most of them that settled here,
   Were from the old Bay State.

On horses' backs the vet'rans came,
   With furniture and store,
Pillion and ample saddle-bags,
   And children—half a score,—
O, could you but have seen them come
   A tracking through the wild,
The father and the mother hale,
   With e'en their sixteenth child!

So earnest, and so merrily,
  Busy as little bees,
A hunting out the lonely way
  By the newly spotted trees—
And when they met a river deep,
  They felled a lofty tree,
And to the children sternly said—
  "The other bank you see!"


Then dived at once into the stream,
  And swam their horses through—
Then cried aloud from yonder shore
  "Child, keep your balance true!"—
And this's the way our fahers came—
  I hope it will be news—
And these the men that built this honse
  With its old—Box Pews.


'Twas Colonel Kidder owned the land,
  And sent the pioneers—
Twenty in number was the band
  He sent the wild to cheer.
One hundred acres was the grant,
  To every settler free—
Where he might raise his humble home,
  And rear his family.


And when they crossed the little stream
  Where we call Water Street—
Says Rounsevell—here, my comrades, here,
  I'll rest my weary feet.

There, where the smoke through logs oft broke,
    A dwelling neat appears,
There Wilson lives and welcome gives,
    Give him a round of cheers.


And Where Old Parson Leslie lived
    With reverence be it spoken,
D. Cooper's store has closed its door,
And all its trade is broken.
*The good old Leslie.*—Let me rest
    And breathe his sacred name,—
His voice once hallowed all this house,
    He blessed and blessings came.


That good old man! his children rest,
    Sleeping beneath the sod,
Save one, and blessed be her name,
    She walks on earth with God.
His children's children here we see,
    God does his covenant keep
To those who love and serve the lord,
    Their children blessings reap.


But I've digressed—a little on
    There Sampson drove his stake,
And thought by tavern in his logs
    A few more pence to make;
His only son, our good old Squire,
    We've often seen him here,
We laugh and wonder, love and mourn,
    And drop at last a tear.

Then farther up beneath the hills;
  There Simeon Farnsworth stood
And looked abroad upon his lands
  And called them very good.
His daughter blesseth now my home,
  Bowed is her aged form,
Calm is her life and sweet her cheer
  As sunlight after storm.


Then out upon the spreading hills
  There Safford took his seat,
And Farnsworth, father of the sons
  Whose names we all repeat;
That good old patriarch famed of old
  For stories doubtful true,
Such as of "Salmon" in his boots,
  Full sixty pounds he drew;


And once, while passing through a wood,
  Perceived a bear in chase:
Seeing at length a hollow stub,
  He sought its hiding place;
But nothing daunted was the bear,
  The stub he clambered through,
And, seated on the old man's head,
  The bear was hidden too.


Thrice round his hand the bear's *tail*
  He drew with tightened grasp,
Then pricked his seat, they upward leaped,
  And breast to breast they clasp.

They fought at length an hour or two
    On top that hollow stub,
When, all at once, he knocked him off
    And killed a bear and cub.
This Farnsworth, father of the sons
    Whose names we all repeat,
To sixteen children he was sire;
    To mention him was meet.


Daivd and Daniel, Reuben too,
    They lived and labored here,
They worshipped with us 'neath this roof,
    We tasted of their cheer:
Comes not the Deacon at this hour
    Our festival to bless?
Methinks I see him everywhere,
    As close around we press.


I hear his snuff-box— rap, rap, rap!
    His hand I'm grasping too,
His anecdotes are passing round,
    His listeners not a few:
His voice was loudest in the throng,
    We all his step could hear;
He loved to sing a christian song,
    And in the front appear.


Peace to his ashes! let him rest;
    His life with us began;
If he had frailties, let *them* rest,
    He lived on earth a— man.

There to the right was Burbank's place,
    Old Jacob, was his name,
His sainted children dwell with us,
    He has his share of fame.

To liberty, he gave a son;
    To men, fond matrons true;
To church, he gave a minister,
    And a good Deacon, too.
Then, farther on, down Lowell sat
    Among his youthful throng;
'Mid nature spurred by poverty,
    They grew up brave and strong.

His son, old Simon he was called,
    When he was passed his teens;
He thought to take to him a wife,
    And paid the priest in *beans*.
As no man of his early lot,
    How lowly it be named,
Need ever blush if he is not
    Of his own self ashamed;—

So their decendants, here to-day,
    So lavish of their means,
Do bless in heart, with honest pride,
    *The bushel of white beans.*
Still farther down to Lempster street,
    Went Spalding bustling round,
A fat old burly gent was he,
    In fame he stands renowned.

He was not called a glutton, sure!
    Yet fondly loved his mouth;
One meal he ate twelve pounds and more,
    And never spoke of drouth.

"What news from court?" he said one day
    To Penniman esquire,
"What news from court?" have you heard say,
    Or why do you inquire?
To one boiled pudding, one small peck
    Of Indian meal they say,—
"Hold! hold my friend!— then I will have
    Full half a score a day."

His dear good wife for Johnny-cakes
    Was noted, so they say:
She lived more than a century
    And died but yesterday.
But do I tire while tattling on,
    And think I'm telling news,
While I am telling where they lived
    Who built the old Box Pews?

Then come along, while I lead on,
    Toward the south we'll stray;
A man of sense and skill we find,
    Old Captain Brockaway.
He built the mills, the merry mills,
    That ground their wheat and corn;
He sawed the logs that built the homes,
    Where our good sires were born.

Plump up beside the Millin pond
   I Captain Proctor see;
He served the town with good renown,
   A rough old man was he.
His father sent a note to church
   One hundred years before,——
A child is born—the mother safe,—
   Praise God and him adore.


There out across the wood and stream,
   Sat Danforth, fat and fair;
A wife he had of rubies' worth,
   Of worldly goods his share.
Is our good Jonathan, his son,
   Like one of that fond pair,
Whose love was wonderful, 'twas said,
   Surpassing e'en the "fair?"


His present wife a Draper was,
   We fondly love her still;
Her ancestors here lived, and gave
   Their name to yonder hill.
Then up along the "Barney hill"
   The Barneys sowed and reaped;
Their children's children well indeed
   Have their possessions kept.


The Tabors—well our native town
   May these mechanics boast—
Their skill and numbers, counted o'er,
   They counted well a host.

There, crown upon the highest hill,
    Sat Healey's seat of yore;
His children taught the rising youth
    From books the hidden lore.


And one yet lives whose snow-white locks
    Among us could we see,
How willing would this brilliant throng
    With reverence bow the knee.
He taught our fathers in their youth,
    He taught *us* in his age,
Not from the same old books of yore,
    But from his own life page.


We've heard his voice in "Senate Halls,"
    In "Council rooms of State,"
His form majestic, and his words
    Rest with the good and great.
In christian worship here with us,
    His form we always saw;
He followed close the "golden rule,"
    Love was his book of law.


We love him for his simple truth;
    And they may doubt who can,
That H-o-n., before his name
    Stands there for *Honest Man.*
His honored wife, our President,
    Our monitor, in truth,
Her heart so faithful, large and kind,
    Lives a perpetual youth.

Work is the motto of her life:
　　With hands, with heart and soul:
For home, for man, for God to work,
　　To work for the great whole.
I've led you on to Stoddard line:
　　Now, Westward, Westward ho!
There stands the Colonel hat in hand,
　　With graceful bow and low.


A good old man was Colonel Wright,
　　A little vain, 'tis true,
As he told o'er his martial feats,
　　Or rode at a review.
A little story I'll repeat,
　　The fight was with a bear;
"To look a Major in the face"
　　He cried "how do you *dare?*"


That he was brave as well as bold,
　　Each child has learned to know:
The courage that could face a bear,
　　Had faced his country's foe.
So long as this fair temple stands,
　　And worship rises here,
That Book,* a present from his hands,
　　Shall witness to him here.


Those good old men! those granite men!
　　I cannot name them here;
I cannot tell their virtues o'er,
　　I only can revere.

　　　　*A Bible for the pulpit.

I've told you much, I'll tell you more,
   (I hope it will be news;)
Of how they built this house that held
   The old—Box Pews.

Our Pilgrim fathers loved their God;
   Their worship was sincere;
So our forefathers knelt to him,
   And built this temple here:
In seventeen hundred eighty-seven,
   This building was begun;
'Twas finished seventeen eighty-nine.
   For so the writings run.

The timber grew near Island pond:
   They drew it many a rood;
The love of freedom and of God,
   Their murmuring all subdued;
They came in shirt and frock, home-made,
   Their feet all brown and bare;
Their breakfast was of bread and milk;
   This was their choicest fair.

Here let me stop and rest a while,
   Where *purpose*, high and strong,
Could poverty and want defy,
   And triumph with a song!
They all united, heart and hand,
   Their workmen were, each man,
Some chopp'd the wood, some scored and hew'd,
   And some could draft and plan.

These men of granite, granite brought;
   *Nerve* spoke in eye and tone;
In hope, and faith, and trust, they placed
   The firm foundation stone.
And when the sills thereon were placed,
   And all the sleepers in,
The sprites and fairies claimed the house
   Their revels to begin.


Mild Evening drew her curtain brown,
   And shut the day from night;
Young men and maidens gathered there,
   And danced till morning light.
That very day the "Raising" came;
   From all the country round
Boys, men and matrons gathered there,
   With cheer and plenty crowned.


They brought the fatted calf, and lamb:
   They brought their pewter too,
Barrels and tubs of home-made beer,
   And baked beans not a few.
They brought, with great brown loaves of bread,
   Puddings and pumpkin pies;
They brought the exercise and health
   Where true enjoyment lies.


Though temperance now rules the house,
   My tongue will not keep mum,
One barrel by the town was bought
   Of good New England rum.

Thus flanked by beauty, love, and cheer,
  The "Raising" they began,
And he who did not do his best
  Was not in fact a man.

The long broadsides being prepared,
  The "raisers" gathered round,
And stood with brawny muscles bared
  To lift them from the ground.
Some stood with pike-poles in their hands
  To aid when needed most;
Others— the strongest of the band,
  With bars to hold the posts.

Old Cummings bustled here and there
  To see if all was right,
Then took his station on a log,
  And cried with all his might,
"Now, *All together; Right up with it.*"
  "Up with it:" echoed round;
Muscles of flesh seemed changed to steel,
  And broadside left the ground.

The pikes were plied, while many cheered,
  And strong men showed their might,
Slowly the long broadside was reared,
  And proudly stood upright.
Now panting, wearied, down they sink
  To rest a little while;
Sweethearts and wives brought in the drink,
  And cheered with word and smile.

Once more they bent their sturdy frames,
   And grasped with iron hands
The other side, and placed it where,
   E'en now, it firmly stands.
The crossbeams then were quickly raised,
   The tenons entered in,
Fitted was each one to its place,
   And fastened with a pin.


Old Cummings still went hurrying round,
   Some say they heard him swear,
That every joint he ever framed
   He knew would pinch a hair.
Slowly the rafters then were raised
   From off their grassy bed,
And placed where only those could go
   Who kept a steady head.


Firmly they placed this noble roof,
   And pinned and braced it strong,
To shield its sturdy worshipers
   From fiercest winter storm.
The old junk bottle followed up,
   Up, up to the tip-top,
And there across the lofty ridge,
   Was drained of every drop.


The day now closed with sunny smiles
   That lighted all the sky,
From hill to hill, from earth to heaven,
   Sweet evening notes reply.

The woodsman sought his humble home,
  His sleep and quiet rest;
His wife beside him slumbers there,
  Her baby on her breast.


And Night, with foot so warm and soft,
  Has hushed the wood and rill;
And life has closed its beating heart,
  And all the world is still.
I've told you how the house was raised,
  I hope I've told you news,
This house that held but yesterday
  The old—box pews.


The morning comes, while labor brown
  Rejoicing hails the day,
And cheerful feet their steps repeat
  Till evening closes grey.
But now the men, the granite men,
  Whom you have heard me call,
Are passing off the stage, to make
  A kind of new subsoil.


Now out upon the rising stage
  Stands Penniman Esquire:
His heart was large, his hands were warm,
  His soul was nerve and fire.
Of all the offices to give
  The town had in its trust,
He all received, and buried not
  One talent in the dust.

He lent the town one hundred pounds,
   To build this house for you;
The oil and paint, the glass and nails,
   He also furnished too.
He freely gave his vote for schools,
   To see was much his dread,
Heads without learning; but much more,
   Learning without a head.


He willed our schools a little fund
   Out of his wealthy store;
And this one liberal act shall keep
   His name forever more.
There's one Tom Brown of some renown,
   Who sold both tape and pop;
Twas the first store, and kept of yore,
   Near French's tailor shop.


And Dr. Harris; bless his name;
   His mission was divine:
He came into this wilderness,
   To pour the oil and wine.
Full forty years he labored here,
   Our native town to bless,
To guide our councils, and to heal
   All sickness and distress.


My childhood well remembers him,
   I hear his calling sound,
"Come, eat the sugar, eat, my dear,
   For grandsir's got a pound."

I've named the Doctor, merchant, Squire,
    But yet no *Lawyer* see.
Was it because they were so poor
    He could not get his fee?

Or was the cause, they sat beneath,
    (I hope this wont be news,)
The droppings of the sanctuary
    In the old Box Pews?
The Farwells, Frenches, Faxons too,
    The good old Azariah,
Though he could pinch a nail in two,
    Was seldom called a liar.

The Beacons, Bloods and Davises,
    The Dinsmores, Smiths and Steels,
And many more, a countless throng,
    My memory not reveals.
I know, indeed, your tired, my friends,
    I'll make a little pause;
I've told you of the men, my friends,
    I'll tell you of their laws.

If any man came here to dwell,
    And poor he chanced to be,
He had his warning to depart
    With his whole family.
T'was 14 days the warning said,
    So said the government,
Was he so low no goods to show,
    When pushed, he pulled and went.

They voted that from May the 10th.,
    To October some day,
No swine should wallow in the mire
    Of the great public way.
They voted 17, 78
    A bounty on each head,
Of 4d sterling, so I find,
On each old Blackbird, dead.


Of pounds they voted fifty-five
    To pay the priest his due,
Said pounds be paid in rye and corn,
    Pork, beef and clothing too.
The price of each was specified,
    From which could none demur,
Except the clothing, which I hope
    They gave the minister.


Now come my friends, this temple in,
    I hope to tell you news,
Something of how it looked within,
    When it held the old Box pews.
The front was then a double door,
    Old fashioned like my own,
And every step, behind, before,
    Age spoke in look and tone.


This very place we're standing in,
    Was called the old broad aisle;
The pews led off on either side,
    In seried rank and file.

There, high in front, like Sinai's mount,
 Where God revealed His law,
With thunderings from the pulpit heard,
 Did they instruction draw.

Here, at its foot with psalm and book,
 The Deacons prayed and sang;
Along the far off sounding aisle
 The sweet old music rang.
The Deacons? Jaquith was the first,
 (I've not forgot his name,)
For piety he was renowned,
 Deacon his son became;

This Deacon's son (a Deacon too,)
 A Deacon's daughter took,
Old Deacon Millen was his name,
 I see his form and look.
Another Deacon let me name,
 Whose offspring here are found,
Like jewels in a circlet set,
 Closing this temple round.

This Deacon Farwell, known to fame
 For hunting honey bees,
With form so lean, with zest so keen,
 Could scent them in the breeze.
One Deacon more, and I will o'er
 Of Deacons here to-night,
The light is dark, but Deacon Clark
 Has gained at length his sight.

I cannot on—he's grasped my hand—
  No *outward* sense can fill
His soul with thoughts so holy, high,
  So sweet, serene and still.
The Tithing men! the Tithing men
  That sat this seat before,
Were men that kept the boys in check,
  In the days that now are o'er.


They rapped the boys for laugh or noise,
  They rapped the sleepers too,
They frowned on looks not found in books,
  They frowned down blushes too.
Hark! hear the clerk now cry the "bans,"
  "*Hear ye, hear ye, hear ye,*
Marriage intended is between
  J. A. and Miss K. C.


If any man can reason show
  Why John should not take Kate,
Speak now, or ever after hold
  His peace;— *God save the State.*"
I've told you much, indeed, my friends,
  I hope I've told you news
About this house, and how it looked
  In the days of the old Box Pews.


But now I'll tell you why they changed,
  (You cannot hope for news,)
The form and features of this house,
  That held the old Box Pews.

Religion chose sweet Liberty,
   And took her here one morn,
And from their mutual, loving hearts,
   Was Education born.

Religion, bound but by one chord,
   To Theocracy would cling,
And Liberty thus loosened, would
   To Despotism spring.
But Education, strong and bold,
   Will guide both Church and State,
Making them just, wise, good and pure,
   Strong, broad, and firm and great.

And thus the three-fold chord* we find
   United here to-day,
Shall bless, shall strengthen and refine
   Our country's Liberty.
The good old men, the granite men,
   Who sped both pen and plough,
They were a *fact* but yesterday,
   They are a *memory now*.

I've told you many things, my friends,
   I hope I've told you news;
O, never let forgotten be
   The days of the old Box Pews.

---

*The House is divided into three compartments, Town House, Church and Academy.

## An Indian Maiden's Lament
### TO THE SACO.

A maiden came with a queenly air;
Her eye was dark, and dark was her hair;
On the rocky bank of her own fair stream
She sat her down for a one last dream.

                        [rushed,
O strong were the thoughts o'er her bosom that
A moment she spoke, then was silent and hushed;
But I caught up the words of her wild, sweet lay,
Borne on the breeze as they floated away.

O Saco, blessed Saco! my childhood's own river!
I've trac'd all thy streamlets with bow and with quiver;
I've tracked the wild deer as he sped to the mountains,
And startled the hare as he laved in thy fountains.

                        [billow,
I've watched the bright flow of each foam-crested
As I sat on the banks and braided the willow;
How bright was the sunshine, how golden its hue,
As I danced o'er thy waves in my birchen canoe.

In thy broad flowing mirror I've braided my tresses,
And bound my long hair with thy wild water-cresses,
And painted my cheek with the breeze from thy waters,
And joyed that they called me a "Brave" 'mong thy
                                   [daughters.

How I've hushed my glad heart and stifled its beat-
To list the glad anthem thou'rt ever repeating; (ing
I tho't the "Great Spirit" would leave thee, no nev- [er,
That I near thy waters should wander forever.

No more, O no more shall the laugh of my brother
Blend in sweet chorus, nor smile of my mother
Light thy dark wave. My tribe have departed,
And left me a lone one —say not broken hearted.

Like thee kindred Saco, I sing in my sadness; [ness.
The pale-face hath wronged me, I yeald not to mad-
My father a chieftain! shall I, his proud daughter,
Stoop to low carnage or think now of slaughter?

I hear thee, obey thee, Thou Great Mighty Spirit!
I haste to the land where my fathers inherit;
Farewell thou blest Saco, I weep and adore thee,
I bow to the warning, and pass on before thee.

---

## OUR BOSTON JOE.

The Sun drives down the glowing West;
The Stage-Coach stops—"Whoa! Whoa!"
And there, mid trunk and box unpacked,
    Unpacks our Boston Joe.

Uncles and Aunts,— Grandmother too,
Welcome the yearly guests.
Grand-father,— he was here but now;—
        Close cousin Joe has pressed.


These heart-felt greetings scarce are o'er,
Ere Joc and Joe are seen,
Arm laced in arm, and homeward bound
        Across our village green.


And seen each day the season through,
Or Sun or storm ne'er fails,
Our Boston Joe at kite or ball,
        Or lounging on the scales.


Or, leading out our Village Boys,
Some fancied foe to dare,
With paper cap and wooden sword,
        So *a la Militaire.*


Or seen at eve sport politics,
From lanterns perched on high,
With Lincoln, Brekenrige or Bell
        Blazoned to catch the eye.


Or angling in the meadow brook
For trout that dart away,
As older Savans oft have found,
        Fishing for what dont pay.

Time steals along, and year by year,
Our Boston Joe has grown
In thought and limb, yet still in heart
    More every year our own.


Beneath the eaves of Fanuel Hall,
The shade of Bunker Hill,
Alternate with our granite rocks,
    His youth was chosen well.


By virtuous talent dignified,
With noble purpose blessed,
We sure shall hear again of Joe,
    Passed manhood's iron test.


You are a builder, choosing now
Materials and tools
For low or lofty character,
    From our New England schools.


Pillar then well with principle,
Humanity at base,
Embracing color, language, laws,
    Extensive as the race.


Carve bold and deep your separate mark
Beside your father's track;
Where Talent shines 'neath Labor's wheel,
    Of Genius there's no lack.

Live not for honors! Do your work;
Count self as second best;
Live for your Country and Mankind,
        And Fame shall tell the rest.

Life is a contest. Should you halt,
Go where your youth was reared;
The Dome, The Fane, the Hills, the Streams
        That strengthened then and cheered.

Oak-Hill and Draper, Lovewell's mount,
The silver, dear Half-Moon,
The little stream that threads the mill
        Shall play the same sweet tune.

The dear old house where Grandsire lived,
The Common, Church and Scales
Shall nerve again your flagging steps,
        And fill your drooping sails

Perchance you'll seek a slender shaft,
And stop as to inquire;
The stone shall answer: "She you seek,
        Dear Joe, has gone up higher."

---

# THY PRESENCE.

Thy presence, O Jehovah,
Guided my youthful feet;
Pointed me then with gentle love
A calm and sure retreat.

Thy presence, through the mazes
Of life's uncertain way,
Whispered a fearless confidence,
And lighted all the way.

Thy presence, when the shadows
Of morning hopes went by,
Strengthened my soul and seemed to say,
Place, place thy hopes on high.

Thy presence, when the sorrows
Of earth came pressing round,
Nerved my bowed heart and gently said,
'Tis for thy good he bounds.

Thy presence, when of kindred,
All, all had passed away,
Breathed of a calm, deep, holy love
That cannot know decay.

## To J. W. S.

I have sent thee a wreath of wild May flowers,
That danced by the stream to the bright, rosy hours;
And I've twined with their beauty a braid of my
To tell how affection lies clustering there. [hair,

O flowers, wild flowers, I've drank from your lips
Love's burning words, as the bee honey sips;
So thou dearest brother wilt read in them there,
A love, a devotion, words cannot declare.

                              [hills,
They will tell thee of days when our own Granite
Breathed the fragrance of love to the green mossy
And bounding together we caught the wild lay, [rill,
Nor heeded the monitor—— Passing away!

The Merrimac laughs, now a fresh, blooming bride,
And sends to the Huron of statelier pride
A flower from her toilet to bloom on her shore,
To hush in the tempest her proud billow's roar.

So I dearest brother have sent thee a flower
To breathe of deep love in thy heart's darkest hour.
Press, press to thy bosom an angel so fair,
It beareth from fond hearts the unspoken prayer.

### I have woven a wreath.

I have woven a wreath,
Come, come to the hill;
I plucked the bright flowers
Beside the cool rills;
Neath the shade of the rocks
That o'er-top the mountains,
Or the silvery rim
Of bright gushing fountains.

Fresh are their petals:
No blight on their bloom.
Their words are of beauty;
Their language perfume;
Joy! joy to the world
Their bright lips are telling;
No sorrow have they
Where sin has no dwelling.

Familiar the places
Where each looked and smiled,
Haunts of my childhood,
When roaming the wild,
Tracking so lightly
The steps of my mother,
Arm linked in arm
With my far away brother.

Friends have departed:
Have fled me and gone.
Home is deserted;
I, I am alone.
"Alone!" hush! ye flowers,
With you? no, never!
Your eyes of deep meaning
Smile on me aye, ever.

Ye tell of a home
In a far distant region,
Bright, beautiful spirits,
Whose number is legion;
The joys of that world
Your bright lips are singing;
Come, come to thy rest,
Thy frail bells are ringing.

---

## I MISS THEE MY MOTHER.

I miss thee my Mother, I miss thee at morn;
When the light steals out, and the day grows warm;
I miss thee at evening, I miss thee at night,
When the Moon shines clear, and the stars grow
                              [bright.

I miss thee, I miss thee my slumbers to break
With thy soft, warm kiss when morn bids me wake,
How often thou'st told me the "Larks in the sky;"
Sleep—let me sleep! 'tis their soft lullaby.


O! I miss the deep love that watched o'er & smiled;
That glad'nd my pathway, that blessd me, thy child;
That tau't me sweet lessons of hope and of trust;
That bade me be humble, for man was but dust.


How often together we've sang the glad hymn;
Thy voice led the chorus, then kneeling to Him,
Thou prayedst with fervor to guide us aright;
Then softly and sweetly we heard thy "good night."


I miss thee my Mother! when weary, oppressed,
Thine arms were around me, my pillow, thy breast.
Now far from thee, Mother, with no one to care,
Where shall I find shelter! O where! tell me where!


Soft breaks on the stillness a deep earnest voice;
I hear it, I've heard it; it bids me rejoice:
'Tis thy voice, my Mother, that wingeth the air,
Beseeching of heaven to shelter me there.

## IMPROMPTU.

Who in winter's dreary hour,
When the merry winds have power,
Who will soothe the passing hour
                Like thee, Brother?

Who to heart will fondly press me,
In his arms so kindly bless me,
When the shades of grief oppress me,
                As thee, Brother

Who will tell me stories true,
Pictured forth in every hue,
With the tact I find in you,
                Dear Brother.

Who will hear me when I sing
Songs of love or any thing
To lighten Old Time's weary wing?
                I know Brother.

Can I touch the light guitar,
Now that thou art gone afar?
No! Its melody would jar
                Without Brother.

## STRAY THOUGHTS

Written at midnight in sickness.

'Tis Night.— Soft slumbers long
Have hushed the buisy throng:
   I wake to weep;
Now softer, sweeter, come
Glad visions of my home—
   I would not sleep.

I tread again its hills,
And track its mossy rills
   With footsteps light;
They come, the glad, the gay,
All centered in one ray
   Of penciled light.

I hear my brother's voice,
I laugh, exult, rejoice,
   'Tis he! 'Tis he!!
And sister, sweet and fair,
We've played full often there,
   I gaze on thee.

Mother, thine earnest look,
That ever from me took
   Sorrow and care,
Seems resting on me now;
It cools my fevered brow
   With its hushed prayer.

O the glad, yearning breast,
My pillow of unrest,
  No power can chill;
I feel its warm embrace,
There— Press to mine thy face;
  I would be still.

I've been so long alone,
So little joy have known,
  I would come home.
Mother! Oh, tell me where
Our dwelling! 'tis not there;
  Must I still roam?

Still seek from bird and flower,
From teinted skies and shower
  A love not there?
As though a wood or rill
 *With love a soul could thrill,*
  Or list my prayer.

Must I still roam? O tell!
Thy look is a farewell;
  I am alone.

* * * * * * * * * * *

No! not alone, above
I turn with yearning love,
  And eager press
With joy that brighter shore,
Where partings rend no more,
  Where love doth bless.

## I WISH I WERE AGAIN A CHILD.

I wish I were again a child,
On whom a mother fondly smiled,
    And told of legends hoary;
O that blessed place upon her knee,
Her dark eye fondly blessing me,
    All know a mother's story.

Or, pleased no longer with a toy,
I would I were again a boy,
    O'er hill and wild-wood bounding.
From the tall pine-top's shady crest,
Where the bold eagle builds her nest,
    My fowling-piece resounding.

Or launched upon the billowy sea,
O'er mountain waves, the bold, the free,
    My frail boat stoutly guiding,
I loved to battle with the tide,
Where breakers roar, my skiff to guide,
    Their fury joy out-riding.

Again on man-hood's verge I'd be,
Where Science says to soul "Be free,
    Go evermore exploring."
I'd scale the mountain's rocky height;
To the bright heavens I'd wake the night,
    With rapturous thirst adoring.

But now how humbled is my lot;
Though doomed, in seeming, here to rot,
    This dumb machinery plying.
Hope spreads her wings above its roar;
On strengthened pinions out I soar—
    Is not the soul undying?

Say ye with millions in your purse,
I, drawn on poverty's low hearse,
    Have ye e'er heard me sighing?
Tell that beside ye I have stood,
And battled for the true, the good,
    From danger never flying.

Can a pure, high heart ever quail!
'Tis *erring* makes man weak and frail,
    And sees him meanly cowering;
A blessing meant us when, O Earth,
Thou with a struggle gav'st us birth!
    Struggle! 'tis greatness towering.

Be calmed my burning heart, be still;
Love, suffer, bear, endure of ill;
    There comes a glorious morning;
They shall not say when I am dead,
"He crouched to power and bowed his head"
    Where his proud soul was scorning.

Now welcome life, or welcome death;
'*Tis living right*, not drawing breath,
    That makes up an existence.
What matters who the trappings share,
If hearts but truly shall declare,
    "His life was a consistence."

## TO ELLEN COCKRAIN.

They say thou art departing,
    Our own Dear Nell!
Why many a tear is starting
    Love best can tell.
We'll miss thy quiet bearing,
    Thy smile, too, Nell!
We who are sadly sharing
    This hour's farewell!

We'll miss thy gay laugh ringing,
    *Thy own laugh*, Nell!
A light and gladness flinging
    Where e'er it fell.
The true word kindly spoken,
    We'll miss that, Nell!
The bruised heart and broken
    Have known its spell.

We miss thee ever, ever,
    Our own dear Nell,
Forget thee never, never,
    No! never, Nell!
Not when the morning waketh
    With sound of bell,
Nor't eve when tired limb acheth,
    Yes, acheth: Nell!

O sad it is this parting,
  This parting, Nell!
I've felt the life-blood starting,
  Thou, God canst tell!
When hand with hand was grasping
  As now dear Nell!
And heart to heart was clasping
  A last farewell.

---

AN INVITATION being extended to the female operatives of Naumkeag Mill to join the floral Procession on this, the anniversary of our National Independence, and being asked why we did not join them, I have related the following in answer.

---

In a splendid, stately dwelling
  Two brothers first saw light;
One to home and high-born station,
  One to toil and night;
They called the father cruel, partial,
  Why this unequal lot?
His way he passed in silence on,
  When questioned, answered not.

Though their paths so marked and different,
  Each aimed high and right;
On a silvery stream one glided,
  One scaled a rocky height.
Ease had made one tender, thoughtless,
  Leaning on some breast;
Toil, the other sober, earnest,
  On himself to rest.

But they looked alike on nature,
  On the sea and sky;
Each had sounded ocean's valleys,
  Climbed the mountains high;
Each had heard the stream's low murmur;
  Where the forest trees
Sing to God their flowing numbers,
  On the evening breeze.

Each had toiled, each in his station,
  Each for home and kind,
But when blessed with power and honors,
  One became half blind;
And he ne'er could see his brother,
  When he passed him by;
And he looked in scornful coldness
  When he came too nigh.

For his hands were rough with toiling,
  And his coat thread-bare,
And he cared not for the smoothing
  Of his matted hair.

But his tones so rough in seeming.
   Told with thrilling power,
All his God-like soul revealing
   In the trying hour.


Once 'twas said the father softened,
   Bade the son return,
For he found a SOUL indwelling
   Where he thought to spurn.
Could that hapless outcast brother,
   Doomed to toil and roam,
Bade return some festal morning,
   Feel himself at home?


So he said in seeming calmness,
   As he turned away,
We have both one earthly mother,
   Both from heaven one ray;
I envy not thy noble breeding,
   All thy pomp and pride,
I walk alone; no servile creeping,
   Or meet thee side by side.

## Soliloquy of the Half-moon.

I'm a bright mountain lake,
Where birds their echoes wake,
Where flowers their shadows make
      Morning and noon;
Where the fringed willows droop,
And the sweet maples stoop,
And vines their tendrils loop
      O'er the Half-moon.

Where the winds merrily play,
And the waves laughing say,
What a glad holiday
      On the old Half-moon;
And the fish sportive leap
Up the green mossy steep,
And then back to the deep,
      To me Half-moon.

Where like a ray of light,
Man o'er my waters bright
Shoots like a star at night,
      In his canoe.
Where the sweet music peal
From the clear ringing steel
Of the swift skater's heel
      Clarrions threw

See! to the distant skies
Lovell and Draper rise,
So works the Wondrous Wise
      From my lowly bed;
Lessons they read to you;
To your own soul be true,
Ne'er ashamed though you grew
      Up in a shed.

When on creation's morn,
With the hills I was born,
Nature's face to adorn
      Ages ago,

I sang the same blessed theme,
Praising the great Supreme,
No human thought between.
   In ebb and flow.


Speak, then, thy Maker's praise,
Through all thy earthly days,
Seeking not others' gaze
   On the good done.
Work for the TRUE and RIGHT;
Work through the dreary night,
Then shalt thou wake in light
   With the "Well done."


## THE YANKEE.


A yankee sat beside his door,
Whistling wild snatches o'er and o'er,
A smile, a frown, his bosom wore,
   "I've cast my lot!"
O stupid fool! O foolish ass,
To think upon so sweet a lass,
Life's but a shadow, let it pass;
   Farewell loved cot."

His hand upon his brow he pressed;
Then turned him to the glowing West,
That only land where souls are blessed,
         And arm is free.
He hewed and whistled, sang and wrought,
Planted and threshed, and sold and bought,
But never touched the thing he sought:
         "Not here," said he.

I'll glory seek— Ho, Mexico!
Thou fabled land, Eldorado,
My crown is won, Palo-alto,
         Call glory bliss.
Call slaughtered sire and bleeding son,
And country wrenched, a victory won?
My country dear, thou art undone
         If glory's this.

He donned his coat. With spade in hand
He sought at once that fabled land
Where gold is mixed with every sand,
         Each rock an ore:
He dug and sifted, washed and dried,
And every new invention tried
To heap up gold, yet ever sighed,
         One nugget more.

"My dream is o'er," the yankee spoke;
"Thrift's deprivation— glory,s smoke,
And gold than slavery's galling yoke
         More subtle far.

It lures us on, a meteor bright;
Nature and God it shuts from sight,
Then leaves us in a moral night,
        Without a star."


He stood, he turned;— O glorious sea!
Upon thy breast again to be,
And with thy waves away to flee,
        This, this is rest.
O, how I've loved the tempest's roar,
That lashed along the rocky shore,
Thy mountain billows white and hoar,
        Then was I blest.


With nerve that ne'er could flag or tire,
With arm of strength and soul of fire,
He sought for something higher, higher,
        His soul to sate.
O'er seas of ice, mid heavens of flame,
He chased afar the fantom, fame,
He called, and lo! the lightnings came
        To call him great.


From Iceland where warm fountains play
Beneath the deep, "peace! lead the way
Far up beyond old Baffin's Bay,
        The open sea.
Around the Pole the lightnings go,
Through Beering's Straits, heigh ho! heigh ho!
The cable's laid to Francisco;
        "What more for me?"

Among the lofty granite hills,
Whose bosom feeds the little rills;
That turn, in turn, the merry mills,
        I saw an open door;
How beautiful those infant forms,
'Tis fireside joys the bosom warms,
As sunlight blessings after storms;
        My tale, dear friend, is o'er.

## AUTUMN LEAVES.

Ye sere leaves of autumn,
That play round my door,
Ye come with a cheering
To the worn and the poor;
Ye tell how a life, when
Its summer has flown,
May bring a rejoicing
Wherever it's known.

Ye mourn not the time when
In sunshine and light
Ye gracefully waved
From yon forest's height;
But ye play in the breeze,
Or chant in the storm,
Or smile in the sunshine,
Though withered your form.

Ye sere leaves of autumn,
Ye live not in vain;
Your worth shall be told
By the frosts and the rain;
When spring shall return
And its fresh airs shall play,
How rich bursts the foliage
Where ye shall decay.

Like leaves of the forest,
The old and the poor,
They close round our hearth-stone,
They circle our door;
O suffer them there, then,
To live and to die,
For blessings like verdure
Shall spring where they lie.

## GONE— MARY A.

Daughter of Wm. P. and Sarah H. Greenleaf, aged 11 years.

On the verge of womanhood,
Pure as any saint she stood,
Gentle, beautiful and good.

Slow she perished day by day,
Slow, wtih canker touch, decay
Reft the bloom of life away.


How we loved her, how we wept,
While the death film dark'ning crept
O'er those sweet eyes till they slept.


Low we bowed upon the clay,
Kissed her forehead, tried to say,
"Wherefore goest thou away?"


And a low voice seemed to say,
"Call me never if you may,
Happier I, than you who stay."

       **FEB. 16th 1863.**

## TO *M. G. on her Wedding Day.

The sources whence our joys we little guess,
Till years of frequence into partings press.
Then like a coil that backward is unwound,
Unthought of memories through our bosoms bound.
Thy voice amid the flowers beside my cottage wall,
The shadow of thy passing in the open hall,
Thy light, quick step across our village green,
The sudden ray of light struck from thy eyelids' screen,
Thy clear, sweet voice amid the holy hours,
Whose notes like dew-drops perfect music showers,
In softened cadence all my dwelling filled,
Soothed my worn spirit, and life's tempest stilled;
These, and a thousand nameless more I'll miss:
But go and shower them, like the winds that kiss
The thousands' cheeks who know not whence the bliss;
Nor be your childhood's scenes or friends forgot
Amid the duties of your woman's lot.
This simple tribute from my heart, I pray
Accept, dear friend, upon your wedding day.

Dec. 19th, 1862.

## TO JENNIE.

O Jennie, dear Jennie,
What, what shall I sing?
Birds sigh in the bowers,
Birds float on the wing;
They're telling their love tales,
O, why may not I?
I lisp and I stutter
Yet, yet I will try.

*Mary Griswold

I'm poor and I'm homely,
Not witty or wise,
Yet sometimes I come
In a sensible guise.
They bid me be gone
Because I am poor,
Because I am homely
They shut too their door.

In youth I loved learning,
Yes, nature and I,
From morning till evening
Together would lie,
She teaching me music
And beauty unseen,
By knight of the ball room
Or long bag of green.

We grew up together,
Twin nature and I,
Yet some how or other,
I often would sigh;
I turned from her beauty,
Sought beauty in mind,
Dear Jennie, 'twas humbug,
I found only wind.

I next sought in fashion,
In wealth, a fond bride;
I laughed at their seeming,
'Twas vanity, pride;
As bees to the flowers,
They after me run,
Why was it dear Jennie?
I sat in the sun.

I then sought in heart,
My idol to find;
I pleased while I flattered,
Their faults cast behind;
But when they should sacrifice
Any thing dear,
They cried in astonishment,
Hear, only hear.

But soon I grew wanton,
And each maid I saw,
I said in my heart, sure
In HER is no flaw.
From poverty's darkness,
Through penury's vale,
To where the proud mansions
Of luxury hail,

I sought a devoted
Affectionate wife,
Whose heart was not selfish,
Whose tongue had no strife;
Whose eye with no malice
Or envy would leer;
On a rival could look,
Dropping only a tear.

I found her at last,
She wrought by my side;
So much like twin Nature,
I knew not my bride;
So noiseless and calm,
But O, when she smiled,
There beamed with an angel's
The trust of a child.

Her I clasped in a close,
Still a closer embrace,
She hid in my bosom
Her sweet, angel face;
Twin children of nature,
I said with a sigh,
We'll travel together,
My Jennie and I.

## PICTURE NO. 2.

Died at Washington, Cora, daughter of
L. and G. Beckwith, aged 17 months.

How beautiful! exclaims the passer by,
And stooped and wondered as the face drew nigh;
Large eyes and brown, so full of softened light,
They seemed like stars that shine to us through
The large, broad fore'ed of transparent hue [night.
Revealed the trickling veins of heavenly blue.

If to a passer by, she seemed so fair,
What to a Mother with her tender care?
The sweet, soft patter on the echoing floor;
The ringing laugh as she climbed up the door;
The mute appeal as she crept near; the kiss;
The tear that called out all the woman, she shall
            miss.

The dear, soft burthen to your bosom pressed,
As, kindly trusting, you laid down to rest;
The dimpled hand that wandered o'er your face,
The fear and darkness from its world to chase.
A watching angel in the heavens is made:
Walk on dear Mother and be undismayed.

By Mississippi's rolling, surging stream,
Where canons roar, and glistning bayonets gleam,
Her Father, watching at the midnight hour,
Shall see in heaven his own, sweet garden flower.
War's foul embrace, nor comrade's clotted gore
Shall stain nor fright.— His child has gone before.

JAN. 18th. 1863.

## MORNING.

Morn broke upon a scene of beauty;
For Night had mantled the earth in soft snow,
And the warm south had garlanded it with beauty.
Forest and upland, the stately pillar,
The old farm fence and the humble dwelling
Of the poor man, with a quick eye, she had
Festooned with glittering frost work, and flung
O're all a silvery vail of gauzy mist.
No breath stirred the quiet, save where Robin,
Who from its northern home had come lighting
Upon a bough, sent down a brilliant shower
Of feathery whiteness; or chickadee,
Who at the accustomed door where child-hood
Threw it crumbles, uttered its simple name
In cheerful music.

MARCH, 1861.

## MY SCHOOL DAYS.

O, my school day tasks are over,
Hurrah for the hill and lea;
My school day toils are over,
And I'll sing right merrily.

They tell me of old Parnassus,
And the skill of the wondrous nine,
But better I like my fowling piece.
And a partridge on yonder pine!

Grand they have taught me to call it
On stump or in forum to spout,
But better I like on the mossy sod
To angle for perch and trout.

They tell me of ladies and beauty,
And eyes they call "killing bright."
More telling to me is the dew drop
That sparkles in morning light.

But my school day tasks are over,
Hurrah! I am free, I am free!
But my school day joys, are they over?
My friends, are they leaving me?

What a fool, what a tool the heart is,
That beateth to every tune;
Frozen now by a breath from January,
Then melted by a glance from June.

No, not are my school days over;
My teachers so noble and true,
Like the harp in the hands of Appollo,
E'en the stones after them drew.

No, not are my school days over,
There's Arthur and Ben and Ham,
And Joseph and George and Webster,
And Maurice and John and Sam,

And Nellie and Jennie and Mary,
And Lucy and Emma too,
And Clara, Mariah and Helen
Are some of a chosen few,

                                   [ty,
Who lighted these halls with their beau-
Their wit and their noisy glee;
No, not are my school days over
At Tubbs Union Academy.

## Crossing the Rappahannock.

One! two! three! tolled the hour of the morn;
And ravine and river lay wrapped in a cloud
Of soft flowing mist from the heavens that bowed,
As silent lay sleeping as death in its shroud.
Two! three! four! Now like specters are seen,
Soft parting the mist on the river and shore,
The busy bridge-builders, the engineer corps;
The river slept on, though pontooned half way o'er.
Three! four! five! tolled the hour. Boom! boom! boom!
And thousands leaped up as the signal was made,
And instant, whole volleys its mandate obeyed;
So murderous the fire, the bridge in mid-current stayed.

And still hugs the mist to the
   river and shore;
And still the sharp-shooters their
   death-dealing pour;
Still hoarse growls the cannon
   with murderous roar,
And the unfinished bridge in mid-
   current wore.
Eight! nine! ten! tolled the hour
   of the morn;
From cellar and stone wall, from
   rifle-pits came
The rebel's cold steel with a mer-
   ciless aim;
And the gallant New-Yorkers, the
   engineer corps
Lay silent and bleeding on river
   and shore.
Cried thousands of voices in one
   loud acclaim,
SHELL THE TOWN: and from Burn-
   side the grand order came,
"Concentrate your fire and shell
   out the city!"
One glance— it is past; for war
   has no pity!
From left, right and centre, two
   hundred guns roar,

A tempest of thunders shakes mountain and shore.
The heavens seem rent, and the broad livid flash
From the foul cannon's mouth reappears with a crash
O'er the doomed city, that hurls from its walls
Back in proud echoes defiance that palls,
As they beat up the bluffs of old Falmouth and bound
Far o'er the town. From the hills all around
Swell back the echoes, repeat and encore,
While the batteries incessant their shot and shell pour,
Confounding confusion with terrific roar.
A silence, a signal, deep, dread and profound
Rose blank on the ear, stopped the blood in its bound;
Tossed, torn in the tumultuous ocean of sound.
Now, fiery and red, struggles up the great Sun,

The shadows uplift, and the mists scud and run;
Huge columns of smoke now commingling lower,
Now packed into blackness, a monument tower
Aloof o'er the city. A moment, and there,
Amid a sirocco of sulphurous air,
Lay Fredericsburg utterly dessolate, bare,
Save the leap and the crackle of flames, and the hiss
Of the burning; a warning with traitorous kiss,
As they stretch like a giant and lick up the snow
On the roofs, a drop in their torment of woe.
Meanwhile the bridge-builders, their efforts essayed;
Still the rebel sharp-shooters fire on undismayed,
And the unfinished bridge in mid-current stayed.
"Who'll clean out the rebels?" says Burnside, hear! hear!

Who heeds death nor danger, and never knew fear
When his country demanded? Who'll volunteer?
Then outsteps Colonel Hall of Fort Sumpter fame—
The 7th Michigan, 19th, 20th I'll name;
Of old Massachusetts, but a handful remain,
And the deeds of their comrades they never will shame.
There firm in the front, they motionless stand,
Their life for their country, they wait but command.
As the firm granite rocks, that lowest of earth,
Some earthquake upheaval gives nobler birth,
Transforms into mountains, majestic and grand,
By tempests unshaken, power's might can withstand,
So stood in their manhood, this brave little band.
They rush down the bank, but a moment they hover,

And play at sharp-shooting, their
foe to discover;
Now they dash for the boats—
Push away boys— away!
Pull the ore, nerve and muscle,—
Hurra! Hurra!!
Crack! Crack! go the rifles, and
close to the water
The Rebel death-bullet sped hun-
gry to slaughter;
Their work is well done—Now se-
cession never!
Away! pull away boys, the union
forever!
They gain the mid-current and
stretch for the bluffs,
Pull away with their hail, though
the river is rough;
Like deer they shall leap when
our powder they snuff.
The 7th are in safety; the breath-
less suspense
Of the thousands on shore, with
a thrill as intense,
Bursts in one long shout of exult-
ant applause;
A deed so heroic, to majesty
awes.

The oars-men, they slake not a
    moment their speed;
They see but a moment their
    comrades who bleed;
'Tis for liberty, freedom,— the
    white as the slave;
The stars and the stripes o'er their
    country to wave.
How nobly they press! Massachu-
    setts' boys strain;
The death-dealing bullets are show-
    ered round like rain.
Hurra! it is ended; they leap for
    the shore;
The rifle and carbine are grasped
    for the oar.
They rush up the steep; for the
    rebels away,
Ye gallant New Yorkers, they've
    paved well your way.
Have a few noble souls, more than
    batteries loud,
Or tons of hot metal our enemies
    bowed.
Exult, ye proud Mothers, But
    yester-day morn,
They said with rejoicing, a man-
    child is born.

To-day, to your sons a nation gives birth;
Aye, more: they do count with the noble of earth.
What though with your life-blood Rappahannock is red,
Shall more of your sons by their daring be led,
Till victory shall follow the wake of their tread.
Then put off your mourning, and silence your woe;
The lesson was needed—"To trust as we go."
'Twas their garments they threw off, to tell to the crowd
The souls of what heroes our armies enshroud.
Did ye think as they moved their frail skiffs on the lake,
Tossed the rough shining oar, or hacked the pine brake,
Or dared the white surf of the Marblehead rocks,
Filled Boston and Salem with miniature docks,
Or fished on the banks of the Nantucket shoals,

They should lead in the list of
    our heroes the rolls?
Take courage, then, Mothers, pro-
    phetic I see;
They shall count up in millions
    like these that shall be;
And brace up your strength, O my
    country, and dare
In loosening oppression, "ITS PER-
    ILS TO SHARE."
The Lakes of the north cry aloud
    to the Sea,
From Ocean to Ocean our land
    shall be FREE.
Rejoice, Massachusetts, and shout,
    Michigan!
The deeds of your heroes are
    blazoned forever;
Rappahannock repeats them, each
    wave of her river
Are stars on your Escutcheon.—
    A glory forever.

        WASHINGTON, JAN. 1ST, 1863.

## MY OLD COTTAGE HOME.

Written for my Nephew, Z. W. W.

Ye Flowers from my Birth-place,
And grases that grew
By the door of the dwelling
My foot-steps that woo,
I crop ye. Bear, bear
On your Leaves and your Petals
The sweet Mountain Airs,
The Hills and the Streams,
And the Dear Little Rill
Of my Old Cottage Home
At the foot of the Hill.

There my Fore-fathers trod;
How dear is the place,
In the turmoil of life,
Where we first start the race;
It is old, it is shattered,
Time cannot despoil:
The flowers I bear onward
Leave roots in the soil:
Still— my heart, it is still
At the Old Cottage Home
At the foot of the hill.

And there was my Grandmother's
Just there, it stood;
The orchard in front,
And there was the Wood.
I see now the Fence
That encircled the door;
The Well at the corner,
All moss covered o'er;
The Spire from the Village;
The hills as of yore;
All, all these I see
Through that old Cottage door.

Ye beautiful grasses
And flowers, that I take
To my far distant home
By Michigan's Lakes,
Ye're not more beautiful,
Bloom not more fair,
Than those that I plucked
On my own St. Clair;
But ye grew by the hearth,
And your roots live still,
By the old cottage door
At the foot of the hill.

WASHINGTON, AUG. 28TH, 1865.

## A POEM:

Written for East Washington Sabbath School Concert, Oct. 5th, 1862.

---

Pure the faith our fathers bore
To New England's rocky shore;
In the shade of Lovell's Mountain;
By Contoocook's silver fountain;
  Humble offerings, Lord, we bring,
  Sabbath offerings to our King.

Earnest hearts, that Thee would know;
Hearts, with love that overflow;
Humble hearts of deep contrition;
Wills, of child-like, sweet submission;
  Faith, Thy promises that climb;
  Hopes, that leap the bounds of Time.

Lisping childhood's youthful years;
Manhood's prime, his four-score years;
Kindred ties of Fathers, Mothers;
Sacred ties of Sisters, Brothers;
  Here in concert speak Thy lays
  In a glowing wreath of praise.

Life's a Meteor! Life's a star!
Shooting through the depths afar!
No! A planet coursing ever!
Rising here but setting never!

Heaven's bright day that wraps from sight
A glorious day without a night!


Up! To labor let us go;
We may save a soul from woe.
Jesus toiled, the darkness stealing
From our world, the light revealing;
 Cannot we some evil quell
 In his name?— a mighty spell!


Each and all of this our band
Wields an influence. Take our stand.
From this church beneath the Mountain,
Love shall flow as from a fountain;
 Wakening all the desert isles
 With ineffible smiles.


Freedom rang! From out our band
Brothers rushed to guard our land;
Here beside us in our glory,
We are telling their proud story;
 Weeping o'er their comrades slain,
 Kindred with us by this chain.


Come not on their dying sight
Their native village, clean and white;
Contoocook with its silvery fountain;
The little church beneath the Mountain;
 Pastor, Sabbath school, and there,
 Music flooding all the air?

When another concert meets,
　　Will it find us in our seats?
No fond face among its Daughters,
No fond Brother from our waters,
　　Gone to that bright, shining shore,
　　To be with us never more?

Lord we pray Thee, be this school
　　Guided by Thy loving rule;
Jesus Christ, Himself, our Teacher;
God's own Universe, our Preacher;
　　Then, beyond these storms and strifes,
　　Take us to immortal Life.

### The Days when we went a Fishing.

A merry maiden went a fishing,
　　A fishing with a net;
This school of fishes I will catch;
　　Now Will, what will you bet?

To gamble is an awful sin;
　　To gamble is to bet;
Leave off this sin ere you begin,
　　While mercy lingers yet.

Now dearest Will, do but be still,
   Forgive your darling pet;
But mind the SEINE the ACTS between,
   I'll catch the fishes, yet.


O, child of sin, what gulfs between
   The theater and cross;
From arts that lure, with smiles impure,
   Turn, spurn this worthless dross.


Peace, my good Will, be gentle still,
   And push for yonder shore,
Stead, steady craft— O, what a draught!
   I'm Peter, only more.


O, is it right, with heart so light,
   To use the sacred word?
When he appears, the saint who cheers,
   Will your "well done" be heard?


Hush, honest Will, is this a gill?
   And this his sailing OAR?
With fingers tight, he's slid from sight,
   And sailed for yonder shore.


And what is this, and this, and this?
   Eel, flounder, perch, and pout,
Slipped your fingers, nothing lingers;
   Hear the waters shout.

Nothing daunted, little maiden
  Seized a hook and oar,
From the waters lightly plashing,
  Out her prize she bore.

Now dearest Will, our basket fill,
  'Twill make a savory dish;
I caught a school, then turned a fool,
  And kept one little fish.

Girl of beauty, cling to duty,
  Heed not many eyes;
He is wealthy, who is healthy,
Good and Pure and wise.

## THE EVERGREEN TREE.

Harp of the wild wood Evergreen Tree,
Sweet is the sound of thy music to me;
Dear as the words which the Mother mild
Breathes in the ear of her sorrowing child.

In childhood's hours how often I strayed
Away from my home to the evergreen shade,
And listened with wild and childish glee
To the plaintive song of the evergreen tree.

In lonely hours thy song was sad,
And joy notes rang when my heart was glad;
When earnest thoughts to my bosom came,
The evergreen echoed back the same.


In its whispering shade I raised my bower,
And a closet made for devotion's hour;
And often there have I bent the knee
In earnest prayer neath the evergreen tree.


I have often fled to its shade so dear,
When friends were cold, and my way was drear;
And then to my aching heart 'twould seem,
No friend was so true as the evergreen.


The maple and oak stand cold and bare,
Like distant friends in the winter air;
But the evergreen never is changed in form
By the summer's heat or the winter's storm.


I have roamed afar with a boy's unrest
O'er the wide spread plains of the fertile West,
And breathed the air of the Prairies free,
But I missed the shade of the evergreen tree.


And oft in my dreams I would seem to hear
The murmur of brooks with their waters clear,
And list again to the low, sweet tone
Of the evergreen by my mountain home.

I have often wished that my home might be
Cheered by the song of the evergreen tree;
And when I died, that I might be laid
In my peaceful grave neath the evergreen shade.

But it matters not where the dust may lie,
When the soul hath fled to its home on high;
I shall rest as sweet should the palm tree wave,
Instead of the evergreen, over my grave.

But dearest to me of the forest band
Is the evergreen tree of my native land,
And ever sweet will thy music be,
Harp of the wild wood, evergreen tree.

## OBITUARY.

Born to a higher life at Washington, N. H. Timothy, son of John and Sophronia Weston, aged 19 years and 6 months. He was the last and youngest of three sons, who, within the space of four years have left them for the "Better Land." They were all in the morning of manhood, just entering upon its duties and assuming its responsibilities.

Virtuous and intelligent, they possessed a refinement of filial and paternal affection that ennobles the noblest of natures.

We sympathize with you, parents and mourners, in your great affliction, as do our whole community. The chords that bound you to your departed children are not broken, only lengthened; and in their gentle drawings, as age advances, you shall hear the spirit voices of your departed, saying, COME UP HITHER.

Up to the heavenly gates with earnest deed
And loving heart and duty done,
Up to our mansion here, sweet sister, come.
Mother, come. Earth is indeed beautiful
With flower and shrub and voice of song;
In heaven perfection dwells; O wait not long!
And Father, good and best, can Earth find rest?
Its joys and expectations wither;
Its glories fade— O Father! come up hither.

## VALENTINE.

I choose thee for my Valentine;
The birds that sing on bush and brake
Some gentler echoes ever wake—
        Will thy heart answer mine?
I ask thy LOVE— yes, bird and flower,
And clinging vine, and twilight hour
        Speak it divine.

I choose thee for my Valentine;
Although some fairer, brighter maid
A spell upon thy heart hath laid
        That rivals time:
Though Nature's ever-varying face
Hath stolen a march upon our race,
        And won the prize.

I choose thee for my Valentine;
I know thy bearing, PROUD and HIGH;
I know the DEPTH of thy dark eye;
        Yet heed it not.
O richer far that fame hath said,
The poor and hungry thou hast fed:
        THE GOOD ALONE ARE GREAT.

I choose thee for my Valentine,
Because I deem thou hast a SOUL,
That knows but one supreme control,
        The TRUE and RIGHT.
Couldst never hang thy head and sigh,
And FAWN and be a LIVING LIE,
        For fame or pelf.

I choose thee not my Valentine(?)
That woman's weakness, or her power
Could charm thy most unguarded hour—
   Yet, I would fondly twine
My arms around thy yielding neck,
O do not all affection check;
   Press light thy lips to mine.


I choose thee for my Valentine;
I send no gay or painted toy,
No foreign aid will I employ
   To win thy heart.
This simple, plain, unvarnished sheet
Will best the leading thought repeat,
   LOVE DWELLETH HERE.


I choose thee for my Valetine;
Though thou shouldst say my verse is rude,
And ruder she who dare intrude
   On Bachelor.
Thou'st pled, I ween, full many a time
A cause of higher, deeper crime(?)
   Plead now for ME.


"She chose me for her Valentine;"
"Her love so cabined, cribbed, confined,
O'erleaped the bound and fondly twined
   With my heart's truth."
O! then, as judge and advocate,
Dear Sir, decide my future fate
   To blend with thine,

  LANCASTER, FEB. 14TH, 1848.

# VALENTINE.

The birds so gay that wing the breeze
And chant their loves amid the leaves
Choose each some gentle mate to-day;
Have I a tongue, may I not say
    Come bless thy Valentine?

Thy Valentine, thou knowest him well,
As whispered words will sweetly tell,
When he has won the fairy kiss
At eve, like THIS and THIS and THIS.
    Again bless Valentine?

Some swain a softer tale may tell;
But can his bosom ever swell
With love more fond and true? for mine
Has lived through absence, change, and time:
    Thou wilt bless Valentine.

I love thee, girl; Nay, do not smile;
My heart was never place for guile;
'Tis not a love whose touch can THRILL;
'Tis deep, but gentle; strong, but still;
    So love thy Vatentine.

And sometimes when he's far away,
Kneel down at eve and for him pray;
At darkest night or radiant morn,
In health or sickness, smile or storm,
    God bless my Valentine.

Thine immage time may not efface;
Thy memory death shall not erase;
In sunny fields and fairer climes,
Where God's own presence ever shines,
  There love thy Valentine.

    LOWELL, FEB. 14TH, 1847.

---

## VALENTINE.

I come, a gallant Valentine,
As you will doubtless say,
To tell a tale of EARNEST LOVE
In my own humble way.

I have no wealth to offer thee,
Honors nor fame nor power;
An honest name, a loving heart,
These are my only dower.

I ask thee not to share with me
A poverty like mine,
A better fortune waiteth thee;
For me a distant clime.

Yet, ere I go, one parting word
To thee I fain would speak;
'Twill ease the throbbings of my heart,
The tear dry from my cheek.

I thank thee for the deep, warm love
All round my pathway strown,
For the sweet, gushing tenderness
Of every look and tone.

I thank thee thou hast been to me
Like Mother fond and true,
Yet, like that Mother loving thee,
I bid a last adieu.

It may be that thou deemest me
A lonely moping child,
Yet, in my heart's own secrecy
Lie feelings sweet and mild.

Thoughts of sweet love and tenderness,
Of deep unuttered joy,
Thoughts of high heaven and holiness,
Sweet themes that never cloy.

In every vale and running stream,
On mountain, tower, and hill,
In the deep forest stern and wild,
In winter hoar and chill,

When spring comes forth in silver buds,
In sunshine and in showers,
When Earth and Heaven are happiness,
And all the world is flowers,

One voice alone is heard and felt,
One hand is ever seen;
It bids me fondly hope and trust;
My all on Him to lean.

Thus all along my earthly road,
'Mid crosses, toils, and pains,
I seek an even, upright heart,
And have I sought in vain?

O! when, in earlier, happier days,
They flattered and caressed,
I nerved my heart, then humbly bowed,
And laid my pride to rest.

It is not wealth or fame or power,
That happiness can bring;
No! these can never have the power
To rob from death its sting.

O! beautiful the pure of heart,
Their home, a heavenly clime;
Though parted here, you'll meet me there,
MY OWN BLEST VALENTINE.

   Written to Mrs. Sarah Allbright,
    LANCASTER Pa. FEB. 14TH, 1848

## VALENTINE.

A Valentine in humble gear
Would tell in song to one most dear
 Of all the wealth he hath;
Undying LOVE, this is the theme,
'Tis the glad name of God Supreme
 That hymns along his path.

I saw the name in childhood's hour,
Written on bud and opening flower,
　　But guessed not what it meant;
I heard it in the rosy dell,
Where the gemmed dew-drops mingling fell,
　　Where reeds their music blent.


I saw it in the arching bow,
Its blending colors brighter grow,
　　Yet, could not it define:
And asked why doth these tendrils fair
Clasp the cold rock with such fond care,
　　Half human, half divine.


O softer, softer, softer still,
From evening airs and mossy rill,
　　And moonbeams mild and fair;
That word with all its magic power
Nearer and nearer pressed each hour
　　Its nature to declare.


I stood by thee— 'Twas but a glance!
Enough! It broke the misty trance,
　　I woke to life and love;
With new-born sense the wood-bird's prate
Seemed calling to its side its mate;
　　Sweeter the coo of dove.


And when the Sun would sink to rest,
Laying his head on Ocean's breast,
　　She blushed more fondly fair,
Or when he smiled along the sky,
The mountain peaks seemed in reply,
　　A softer hue to wear.

And now, dear girl, where e'er I go,
O'er burning sands or fields of snow,
    Where e'er I chance to roam,
I turn to thee in fond embrace,
And every fear and sorrow chase;
    Yes, thou, thou art my home.


I have no gold to offer thee,
Or gems brought from the Indian sea,
    Or talents high and rare;
I have a soul to thee the same.
Not proudly high or weakly tame,
    Call, call it but thine own.


I'll lay thy head upon my breast,
And fondly kiss thee into rest,
    And call thee all mine own;
And thou shalt sing, la-la, la-la,
And I will laugh, ha-ha, ha-ha,
    With joy we ne'er have known.

## VALENTINE.

I am still thy Valentine,
  Bowing at no other shrine;
Of thy face I'm fondly thinking,
All thy love tones I am drinking;
    Soul from soul no force can bar,
    Witness I, from thee so far.

I am still thy Valentine;
Star-like thou dost ever shine,
Through the darkness softly stealing,
All thy precious self revealing;
In the day-light where I roam,
Thou art there my constant home.

How I miss thy dear caress!
Lips that ever moved to bless;
Yes! when shrouded deep in sorrow,
Thou would'st point a happier morrow;
To my side the closer press,
How I miss thy dear caress.

Hear me, thou to me most dear,
I have loved thee many a year;
When we sat beneath the willow,
Rested on the self-same pillow;
I have loved thee many a year,
Am I still to thee so dear?

Dost thou ever think of me
Here beside the bounding sea?
Wishing, wishing, wishing ever
Thou from me might never sever?
Wishing that upon my breast
Thou should'st find thy happiest rest.

Come and bless me yet again,
O how impotent and vain
Is this wild, this mad endeavor
From thy soul my soul to sever;
Say that blessed word again,
We henceforth shall not be twain.

## THE BEAUTIFUL.

The beautiful, the beautiful, it dwelleth every where;
'Tis breathed in lofty senate or childhood's simple prayer;
No spot of earth but beareth some token of the true,
The living, breathing beauty, that erst in Eden grew.

The little wandering snowflake on the rocky mountain's height
Is O! to me how beautiful 'neath the blasonry of Night;
How welcome to the wanderer far from the haunts of men
Has been the simple mosses' cup: it breathes of hope again.

Some little flower upspringing from places foul and dank,
As bright, as purely beautiful as on the violet's bank;
And when the evening cometh, their rosy lips apart,
They read us silent lessons of the good, the pure of heart.

There came a gentle stranger, her
    heart seemed weak and faint,
She spoke it not, she breathed it
    not, she uttered no complaint.
How patiently she labored, I watch-
    ed her as she drew
The mossy threads of finest webs
    with skillful hand and true.

She scorned to be dependent. O!
    that foul word hath stains
Far blacker to the highborn soul,
    than dungeons, racks, or chains;
She scorned to be dependent, let
    that the answer hear,
Why soft and dainty fingers the
    toils of labor dare.

She toiled in silent beauty. The
    cold December's blast
Went moaning by, a herald in
    memory of the past;
Beside her grew a rose tree, its
    tendrils sought the shade,
They seemed to wake in tenderness
    with every breath that played.

'Twas morning time, you all have
    felt that solemn, silent hour,
Ere darkness fades, or light sub-
    lime gilds hill or temple spire;

The heart will gently rise above,
   her eye was following there,
She saw the rose; her heart gushed
   out in ecstacy of prayer.

My Mother! 'Tis thy gentle arms
   are twining o'er my head;
My Father here? Thy spirit too? I
   deemed thee with the dead;
I can but weep, O God of love! that
   hear'st the orphan's prayer;
I see in every climbing shrub Thy
   love and tender care.

The beautiful, the beautiful, it
   dwelleth every where;
'Tis in the busy work-shop, 'tis in
   the viewless air;
No spot of earth but beareth some
   token of the true,
The living, breathing beauty, that
   erst in Eden grew.

www.ingramcontent.com/pod-product-compliance
Lightning Source LLC
Chambersburg PA
CBHW031120160426
43192CB00008B/1057